HEINTZ ART METAL
SILVER-ON-BRONZE WARES

Kevin McConnell

1469 Morstein Road, West Chester, Pennsylvania 19380

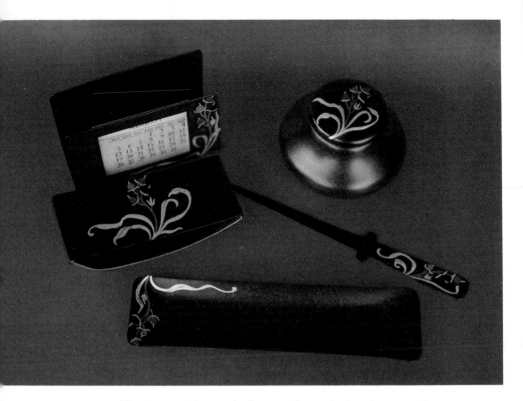

A possibly unique Heintz desk set, where the sterling overlays have been highlighted by cold-painting. The absence of production numbers on any of these pieces strongly suggests that it was a specially commissioned or experimental set.

Published by Schiffer Publishing, Ltd.
1469 Morstein Road
West Chester, Pennsylvania 19380
Please write for a free catalog.
This book may be purchased from the publisher.
Please include $2.00 postage.
Try your bookstore first.

Printed in the United States of America.
ISBN: 0-88740-298-4

We are interested in hearing from authors with book ideas on related topics.

Contents

A pair of rare and unusual Heintz Art Metal wall plaques highlighted with sterling sailing ships. Each plaque is 6¼" in diameter.

Acknowledgments

I am fortunate to own a nice collection of Heintz art metal, but I'm even more fortunate to have friends, family, and acquaintances with similar collecting interests.

It is through their considerable help and encouragement that this book is a reality. All of them went beyond the call of duty to provide me with the information and items necessary to complete my efforts.

I am particularly grateful to Kyle Husfloen, editor of *The Antique Trader Price Guide to Antiques* for encouraging me to write and photograph an article on

Heintz fruit or nut bowl with bulbous body, gently tapering shoulder, and sterling ivy design. 4" high, 8" diameter. Production #3648.

Heintz desk set, nickel-silver plating over sterling and bronze. The pieces in this set include a letter rack (4½" high, 6" long), a rocker blotter (5½" long), a pen tray (9¾" long), a letter opener (9" long), and a set of blotter corners (each 3¾" long). Of the items in this set, only the pen tray and the letter rack have the impressed Heintz mark. Production #1087.

Heintz, which appeared in the August, 1990 issue of that publication. It is through his kind permission that portions of that original research appear in this book.

I am likewise indebted to Bruce Bland, co-curator of The Roycroft Museum, premiere Heintz collector Janeanne Hackley, and Heintz collector/expert Michael L. James for providing me with essential facts and examples for this book.

Last but not least, are the many kind people who shared their time and collections with me. They include: Alvin and Elaine Feit, Linda Feuer, David and Beverly Spillyards, Danielson Antiques, Mr. and Mrs. C.H. McConnell, Sherwood Simmons, Matthew and Beverly Robb, McIntyre's Antiques and Gifts, John Bennett, Mike Pennington, Robert Wyman Newton, Konrad Shields, Wes Miller, and Seymour and Violet Altman.

A Heintz trophy vase with an elaborate windmill and landscape sterling overlay. It is engraved "KEYES TROPHY, MAY 12 1914, AT OAKLAND GOLF CLUB, LOW GROSS, CLASS A, WON BY F.C. NEWTON." The applied medallion depicts a golfer and the words "ENGINEERS GOLF CLUB OF NEW YORK." 11" high. Production #3616A.

Introduction: Rediscovering America's Great Bronze Age

Many years ago, when my collecting interests were limited to wooden primitives, historical flasks, and cobalt-decorated stoneware, I encountered my first piece of Heintz art metal. It was a large vase with an elaborate floral overlay, and a cryptic diamond-shaped maker's mark on the bottom, which no one seemed to know anything about.

Despite the dearth of information relating to this item, not to mention the fact that it did not fit into my collecting scheme, I couldn't help but to be impressed by its obvious quality and beauty.

A Heintz cigarette box with domed lid and strong green patina. Silver overlay of abstract leaves and vines. 3" high, 5½" long, 3½" wide. Production #4106. Also present is the impressed retailer's mark of "OVINGTON CHICAGO NEW YORK."

A grouping of Heintz Art Metal picture frames of varying styles and finishes. 6"—7¼" high, 4¾"—5" wide. No marks.

As is so often the case with collectors, I became rather obsessed with said vase and eventually bought it. And then another one, and another one, and... well, you get the idea. At any rate, I had accumulated a decent collection of these sterling decorated bronzes long before I finally learned that they were the products of the Heintz Art Metal Shop of Buffalo, New York.

Just as there were various art pottery firms operating throughout the country during the early 1900s, there were likewise art metal shops which made decorative accessories from copper, bronze, pewter, brass, and sterling. Unfortunately, these metal shops kept even worse records than the art potteries, making research something of a difficulty.

Nevertheless, I've enjoyed the slow-but-sure process of piecing together the history of this obscure but important manufacturer. For those of you who

are interested in Arts and Crafts metalware, it is hoped that you find this book to be helpful and informative.

I have attempted to achieve many things with my efforts, including the pictorial representation of as many different forms and overlays as possible, in addition to the arrangement of a realistic price structure.

With the current interest in the Arts and Crafts Movement, Heintz art metal is now being recognized as a prominent aspect of the American Decorative Arts. As a consequence, Heintz's popularity is on the rise and examples are beginning to find their places in fine antique shows and important auctions.

As you'll see from the pictures in this book, Heintz's appeal is obvious, and I cannot recommend it highly enough as the most beautiful of investments.

Collect it and enjoy.

Silver Crest cylinder vase with slightly flared, rolled lip. Stylized sterling overlay on textured, silver-plated bronze. 6" high. Production #2042.

Chapter One
The History of the Heintz Art Metal Shop

As the year 2000 looms upon the horizon, the American collecting public has cast its attention back upon the twentieth century, scrutinizing the various decades for interesting and unusual items to accumulate.

Without a doubt, the area which has garnered the most fervent following is the Arts and Crafts Movement; a short-lived period which promoted hand-made, high quality items which were of simple beauty and ultimate function.

The Arts and Crafts era took place from circa 1900 to 1920, with some of its more prominent proponents being Gustav Stickley, Charles Limbert, and Elbert Hubbard and his Roycrofters of East Aurora, New York.

This unadorned bronze box with curled feet and riveted construction is typical of the wares produced by Heintz's predecessor the Art Crafts Shop.

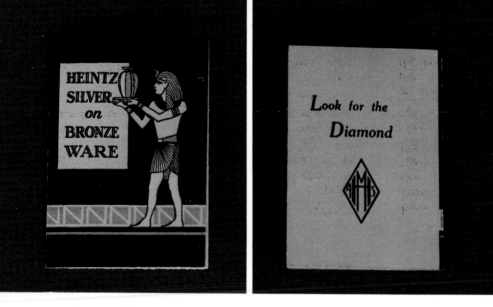

This small booklet (front and back covers shown) was originally included with every Heintz purchase and it contained general information on how Heintz wares were made and how they could be cared for.

Most collectors are familiar with these names as well as with the so-called Mission oak furniture which their firms produced. Because of the current interest and popularity, prices have escalated sharply for most Stickley, Limbert, and Roycroft items. Consequently, many collectors have shifted their sights towards lesser known firms of the Arts and Crafts Movement, who made objects of comparable quality which are still affordable.

One such firm whose wares have been rescued from the realm of obscurity is the Heintz Art Metal Shop. Heintz manufactured distinctive decorative accessories, made in varying shades of bronze and accented with sterling silver Art Deco, Art Nouveau, and Arts and Crafts overlays.

The roots of the Heintz Art Metal Shop can be traced back to 1876 and the Heintz Brothers jewelry manufacturing firm of Buffalo, New York, which was owned and overseen by siblings Charles F. and Louis J. Heintz. As the business flourished and expanded, Otto L. and Edwin A. Heintz joined the family firm at the turn of the century.

Rarely seen are these brass and steel design patterns which were utilized to cut out the sterling overlays.

Otto L. Heintz, founder and guiding force of the Heintz Art Metal Shop. *Photo courtesy of the Buffalo Rotary Club and Michael L. James.*

Although there is no firm evidence to support (or disprove) it, the general supposition is that Otto and Edwin were the sons of the elder Heintz brothers. Whatever the case, it is known that in 1903, Otto L. Heintz branched out on his own to take over a previously established Buffalo metal shop, namely the Arts & Crafts Company located at 391 Franklin Street.

In 1905, Otto changed the name to the Art Crafts Shop, and in 1906 to the Heintz Art Metal Shop, with Edwin joining the ranks shortly thereafter. In 1908, the company was relocated to 1354-62 West Avenue in Buffalo, where it remained in business until the end came in 1929

A Heintz spun bronze vase blank devoid of patina or overlay. 12″ high.

A grouping of Heintz ashtrays with scalloped edges and recessed interiors. Note the absence of silver overlays. These particular examples are marked with the impressed Heintz diamond mark and the words "SOLID BRONZE." 4" diameter. Production #2635.

For twenty-four years the Heintz Art Metal Shop produced objects of beauty and virtue, included among them are ashtrays, bookends, bowls, boxes, candlesticks, card trays, desk sets, humidors, jewelry, lamps, smoking sets, trophies, vases, and more.

As regards the actual procedure of production, round objects were manufactured by the metal spinning process by such men as Henry Eiseman and Peter Dietrich, while flat objects were cut out and formed accordingly. Rough edges and irregularities were then corrected by workers like buffer-polisher Frank Fronkowiak, while George Krollman cut out the delicate silver designs on a giant jigsaw.

These silver overlays were then perfectly bonded to the bronze items through a patented process known as sintering. In simple, non-technical terms, this method involved the very specific heating of the ware, which resulted in the impurities in the silver overlay melting and bonding to the bronze surface.

These two objects exhibit Heintz's great range of versatility and adaptability. Depending upon the needs of the customer, this item was manufactured as either a handled vase or a trophy. The trophy bears an applied bronze medallion/seal of the "ENGINEER'S CLUB, BOSTON" and is engraved as follows: "JUNE CUP 1915, 2nd LOW NET, WON BY C.L. EDGAR." This trophy is marked on the base with the retailer's name—"N.G. WOOD & SON." Both items are 6" high. Production #6571.

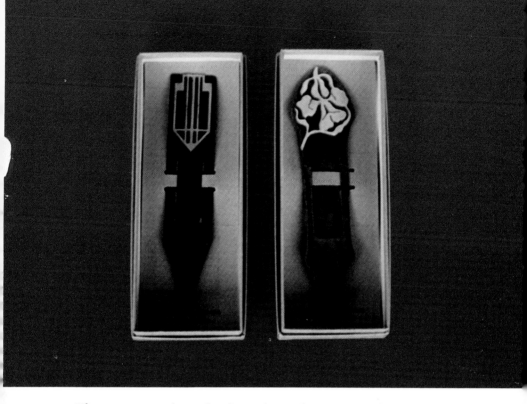

These mint condition book marks in their original boxes are a Heintz collector's dream.

While the Heintz Art Metal Shop remained in business until 1929, the firm suffered a serious setback on January 10, 1918, with the death of its founder Otto L. Heintz. In many ways, this was the slow-but-sure beginning of the end for the Heintz Art Metal Shop.

Without any doubt, Otto Heintz was the driving force and without him things were never quite the same at the Heintz shop. Perhaps it was this very fact that prompted Heintz's head salesman Fred C. Smith to leave the firm in 1919, taking with him many of the veteran metalworkers.

Together, they founded the Smith Metal Arts Company, also of Buffalo, New York, whose early efforts bear a striking resemblance to Heintz's wares despite the "Silver Crest" trademark they utilized during the 1920s.

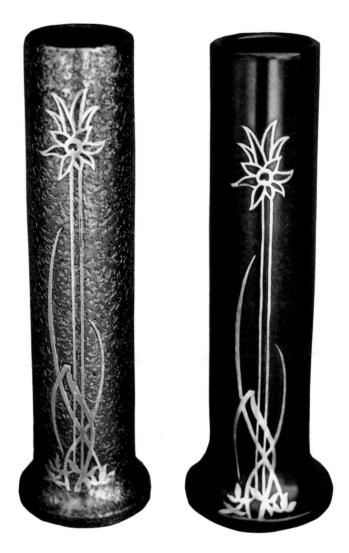

This "pair" of sterling and bronze vases are actually the products of two different firms; the vase on the left is Silver Crest, while the one on the right is Heintz. Judging from these vases, one would have to conclude that when Fred Smith and his group of craftsmen split from the Heintz Shop to found the Smith Metal Arts Company, they took along bronze blanks and sterling overlays. The Silver Crest vase on the left is deeply acid-etched and displays a golden bronze finish, probably to disguise its similarity to the Heintz counterpart on the right. They are each 9" high. The Silver Crest vase is production #8003, while the Heintz vase is production #3736B and bears the retailer's mark of "R. H. MACY & CO."

An extraordinary Heintz trophy cup with dark green patina and heavy silver leaf and vine ornamentation. This trophy is engraved "Second Prize For Decorated Touring Car Won By Rollin B. Mallory. Milwaukee Perry's Victory Celebration. Red, White, and Blue Parade, August 5—1913". 8½" high, 10¼" wide. Production #6530.

Not surprisingly, the Heintz Art Metal Shop felt the dual ill effects of not only losing its top craftsmen, but having to try to compete with them. As the 1920s progressed, Heintz slowly began losing more and more money, finally halting production in 1929.

The stock market crash destroyed any hopes of a comeback, and the Heintz Art Metal Shop officially ceased to exist on February 11, 1930.

Even though the Heintz Art Metal Shop is gone, it will never be forgotten. The Heintz craftsmen left behind an amazing legacy of art objects which are currently beginning to realize the level of value and popularity that they so truly deserve.

By way of a brief history of the Smith Metal Arts

Silver Crest ten-sided pen tray with recessed interior. Stylized bronze floriform overlays on sandblast-textured bronze. 10½" long, 3¾" wide. Production #22060E.

Company, it was originally located on the third floor of a building at Massachusetts and Niagara Streets in Buffalo.

Having set up their new shop, Smith and his metal spinners, design cutters, and buffers and polishers returned to their jobs of making bowls, vases, lamps, trophies, and more. Because of the circumstances, most of these initial efforts would be absolutely indistinguishable from Heintz art metal, were it not for Smith's "Silver Crest" mark.

As the 1920s progressed, the Smith Metal Arts Company relied less and less upon imitation, eventually diversifying its line of bronze wares with a plethora of highly original designs and finishes.

In all likelihood, it was this willingness to experiment and change with the times that kept Smith Metal Arts solvent through the Depression, which claimed so many other firms, including the Heintz Art Metal Shop.

Still in business today, Smith Metal Arts is located at 1721 Elmwood Avenue, where it moved in late 1945. They are currently famous for their high quality desk sets, with some of their clients including but not limited to: Tiffany of New York, Mobil Oil, Henry Ford II, the Duke of Windsor and the king of Saudi Arabia.

The early efforts of this firm are just now beginning to attract the attention of Arts and Crafts collectors. Most examples are as yet reasonably priced.

Chapter Two

A Chronological Study of Maker's Marks

Since recognizing shopmarks is of paramount importance to collectors, this section is devoted to the detailed descriptions of Art Crafts Shop, Heintz, and Silver Crest marks, along with respective representations of them.

Being familiar with these marks is essential, as is being able to recognize unmarked examples which do indeed exist. While most Heintz wares were meticulously marked from 1912 to 1930, the major exception seems to be desk sets which often consist of up to a dozen matching items, with usually only one or two of the pieces bearing the Heintz insignia. The logical explanation for this is simply that the makers never imagined that these complete sets would ever be broken up and scattered hither and yon. Another is that Heintz utilized paper labels, although few have survived the years intact.

Additionally, Heintz and Silver Crest picture frames are never marked, although some examples bear an

Silver Crest inkwell with hinged lid and curvilinear sterling overlay. 2¼" high, 3" diameter. No mark.

impressed production number. Except for a few rare large items, Heintz's sterling and bronze jewelry likewise remained unmarked because of its delicate size. And most of the desk and table lamps encountered, while obviously Heintz and Silver Crest, do not exhibit impressed maker's marks. Lamps were marked almost exclusively with paper labels.

Other unmarked items are occasionally found, suggesting that Heintz and the Smith Metal Arts Company may have had a policy similar to that of the Roycroft Copper Shop, which allowed workers to make items for their own personal use as long as they were not distinguished with the shop insignia. A collection of Heintz objects acquired from the estate of one of their workers would seem to bear out the above theory. Although in various stages of completion, none of the items, not even finished examples, bear any shopmarks.

Probably a product of the Art Craft Shop, this elegant compact is made from enamelled metal with a sterling Art Nouveau overlay. 1½" square, Unmarked.

The Art Crafts Shop

Shopmarks: While a great deal of The Art Crafts Shop output remained unmarked, some of it is clearly identified by a detailed impressed mark. This mark is comprised of the name "The Art Crafts Shop" below which is the designation "Buffalo NY" and still beneath this is the patent date which is represented as "PAT. JUL 21-03. All of this information is contained within an oval reserve.

The period between 1906 (when The Art Crafts Shop became the Heintz Art Metal Shop) and August 27, 1912 (when Heintz was granted his patent for sterling on bronze wares) accounts for the vast majority of unmarked Heintz wares encountered. During these years of transition and pending patents, wares were either left unmarked or were simply impress-marked "PAT. APD. FOR." An impressed production number is sometimes also present.

The standard impressed Arts Crafts Shop Mark.

Transitional mark used between circa 1906 and 1912.

Heintz Art Metal Shop

Shopmarks: The standard impressed Heintz mark is generally found on either the back or the bottom of items, and consists of the overlapping letters "HAMS" enclosed within a diamond. Appearing directly below it are the words "STERLING ON BRONZE PAT. AUG. 27. 12."

Heintz variants made without sterling overlays simply exhibit the Heintz diamond insignia and sometimes the additional impressed block letter designation of "SOLID BRONZE."

As detailed above, Heintz employed paper labels on many of their wares.

The standard impressed Heintz Art Metal Shop mark.

Heintz alternate mark #2. Found on items with acid-etched rather than sterling designs.

Heintz alternate mark #1. Found on items devoid of sterling decoration.

Heintz alternate mark #3. This paper label is to be found on various Heintz wares, particularly lamps.

Smith Metal Arts Company (Silver Crest)

Shopmarks: During 1919 and throughout the 1920s, an impressed circular mark was utilized which bears the trademark Silver Crest in script letters, below which is a squared arrangement of the letters "SMACo." (Smith Metal Arts Company). Furthermore, within the circular reserve is a descriptive designation of the item, such as: STERLING DECORATED BRONZE," "GENUINE BRONZE," "GOLD INCRUSTED BRONZE," or "DECORATED BRONZE."

The standard impressed Silver Crest mark utilized by the Smith Metal Arts Company during the 1920s.

The standard impressed Smith Metal Arts Company mark used after 1930.

From the 1930s until now, items have been marked with the impressed linear block letter abbreviation "SMACo" which is sometimes within a triangular reserve.

As well as the above standard shopmarks, some examples also display the impressed name of the retailer which originally sold the item. Some of those which have been encountered include: "Roos Bros, CALIFORNIA," "R.H. Macy & Co. Inc.," "OVINGTON CHICAGO NEW YORK", and "N.G. Wood & Son." The latter mark is often found on Heintz trophies.

Impressed production numbers are also usually present on most of these bronze wares. In the case of Heintz, one often finds designations such as "404A" with the number indicating the design/shape of the object and the letter representing the style of the decoration. Smith Metal Arts utilized a similar system as well as a hyphenated one, with production specifics appearing as "495—W."

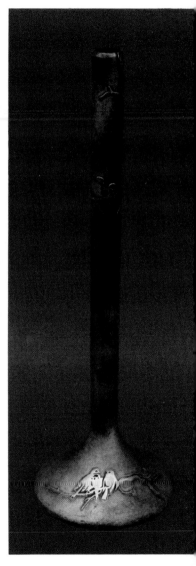

This grouping of 12″ high Heintz stick vases clearly shows the variation in factory patinas. The vase with the brown finish bears the production #3684A, the green vase is production #3684C, and the silver vase is #3684S.

Chapter Three

A Description of Patinas and Surfaces

Detailed below are the different types of patinas and surfaces employed by The Art Crafts Shop, the Heintz Art Metal Shop, and the Smith Metal Arts Company. One will note that there is a greater range of variation and experimentation with the progression of time.

Art Crafts Shop (circa 1903—1906)

This metal shop phase produced decorative and utilitarian brass, bronze, and copper items, which are often unadorned or decorated with simple embossed designs. These embossed designs are sometimes highlighted with colorful enamelling. Some Art Crafts Shop wares also exhibit the striking combination of sterling overlays and polychrome enamelling.

This enamelled dish is a typical example of Art Crafts Shop production. It is 6" in diameter and is unmarked.

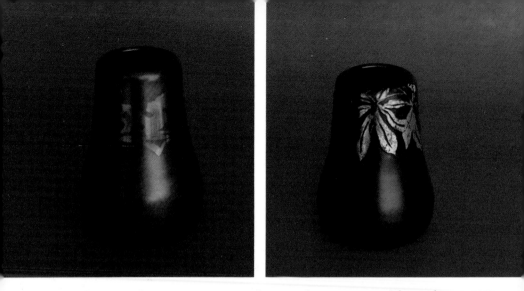

This pair of Heintz vases provides a study in contrast. The early transitional example exhibits a satiny gold surface and an acid-etched bird and wave motif, while the conventional production piece bears a sterling Virginia creeper overlay on dark brown bronze. The early example bears only the impressed diamond mark, while the later piece is fully marked with the diamond insignia and the "STERLING ON BRONZE" designation. Each vase is 3½" high.

Heintz Art Metal Shop (circa 1906—February 11, 1930)

Quoting from a circa 1916 Heintz Art Metal Shop catalogue, the patinas utilized are described in this manner... "Beautiful colored effects have been produced after much thought and experiment, and our efforts are now devoted almost entirely to three finishes, which are as follows:

'Bronze'—A beautiful light bronze color, of softest and most refined color tones.
'Royal'—A deep rich red, with a suggestion of iridescent coloring.
'Verde'—A dark green of varying shades of coloring. This is a decidedly artistic finish."

While the above three were the standard Heintz production patinas, several others were used as well. The most common of these is a nickel-silver wash known as "French Gray", which involved the plating of the entire sterling-on-bronze object. This copied the Smith Metal Arts Company's silver finish, and was undoubtedly intended to compete with it.

Infrequently encountered is a gold-toned, crystalline patina similar to that found on much Tiffany Studios metalware of the period. Owing to the scarcity, one can be certain that this was an experimental line that didn't work out.

Even rarer, is a Heintz variant with an iridescent gold satin finish and acid-etched (rather than sterling) designs, which is most definitely experimental.

Yet another variation involves Heintz wares devoid of any type of decoration. These bear the standard impressed Heintz diamond mark, as well as the designation "SOLID BRONZE." In all likelihood, these are transitional items made shortly after The Art Crafts Shop became the Heintz Art Metal Shop, but before sterling-on-bronze became the standard line of production.

Heintz inkwell with bulbous base, hinged lid, and applied silver medallion. Gold crystalline Tiffany-type patina. 2½" high, 3½" basal diameter. No mark.

Smith Metal Arts Company/Silver Crest (April 24, 1919—Present).

While the Smith Metal Arts Company initially, and perhaps inevitably, emulated Heintz's sterling decorated bronze wares (down to exact shapes, overlays, and patinas in some cases), it is to their credit that they eventually began to experiment and innovate. This resulted in a greater range of textures and finishes than those of the Heintz Shop.

Whereas Heintz's mainstay was sterling-on-bronze objects, Smith's were widely diversified to include not only sterling decorated bronze and the standard silver, green, and brown patinas, but also bronze decorated bronze, a brass finish, a mirror bronze finish, streamlined Art Deco designs without any overlays, and a rare gold incrusted bronze. (It is no coincidence that the latter bears an uncanny resemblance to Tiffany's gold dore, since the Smith Metal Arts Company was contracted by Tiffany Studios to produce this finish for them.)

Furthermore, a plethora of surface textures were achieved by methods as varied as sand-blasting, acid-etching, and submersion in stale beer and sawdust.

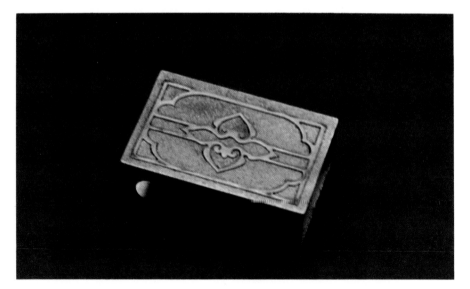

Rarely encountered, this Silver Crest matchbox holder exhibits their "gold incrusted" finish, which they mainly produced for Tiffany Studios. ¾" high, 2½" long, 1½" wide.

Chapter Four
Pricing and Evaluating

Assessing the worth of Heintz and Silver Crest bronzes involves a combination of factors related to the strength of the original design as well as the current condition of the item in question.

There is a great deal of variation as regards these objects, and they should be appraised by the system below before spending any serious money

Patina: In terms of these bronze wares, the type and the condition of the patina are the most vital considerations. Those items with green patinas are preferred by collectors and are worth a 15 to 20 percent premium. Least desirable are pieces with an overall nickel-silver wash; this was a poor aesthetic concept since it erased the intended contrast of the sterling over bronze.

This Heintz cigarette box displays a lovely green patina and a swirling silver overlay, 1¼" high, 4¼" long, 3½" wide.

This is a classic example of the type of Heintz object most sought after by collectors. This vase exhibits a combination of all of the desirable aspects, including a strong form, overlay, and patina, as well as pristine condition. 8¼" high. Production #3840.

Ideally, one wants Heintz and Silver Crest wares with near mint to mint patinas. Unfortunately, a great many of the pieces have been compromised by polishing, which reduces the value by 30 to 40 percent.

Most collectors will not purchase such imperfect examples unless the form or the overlay is extremely unusual. While it is possible to repatinate polished items, the end result can never compare to the original factory finish, which is deep, glossy, and variegated.

Condition: Another important factor is the physical condition of these bronze pieces. There is much evidence to attest that numerous Heintz and Silver Crest objects were, at some point, accidentally dropped or knocked over (particularly tall vases) resulting in dents, bruises, and/or rim damage.

A small dent or bruise will not reduce the value by much—5 to 10 percent at the most. However, rim damage is another matter altogether. Vases and bowls which have been dropped on their rims are usually distorted out of shape due to the force of the fall. There is no way to correct this kind of problem without destroying the patina, thus one is left with a compromised, inferior piece regardless.

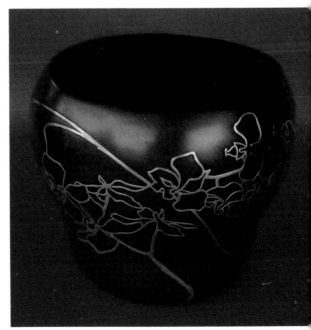

This attractive Heintz jardiniere is an infrequently encountered form. 6" high. Production #3574A.

Heintz cylinder vase with expanded rim and base. Sterling silver Masonic overlay, marked and dated "Pasadena 1913." 6" high. Production #3581.

Again, collectors don't want these examples unless they're something fantastic, and even then, they will only pay 60 to 70 percent of full value.

Form: The Heintz Art Metal Shop and the Smith Metal Arts Company manufactured literally hundreds of different objects of varying shape, size, and purpose. Of primary interest to collectors are strongly designed decorative items such as vases, bowls, and candlesticks, as well as lamps. Of considerably less interest and value are simple, functional wares like letter racks, ashtrays, and pen trays.

Decoration: As is the case with form, there is a great deal of variance in the decorative overlays that appear on Heintz and Silver Crest objects.

Most sought after are items highlighted with sterling silver overlays which exhibit quintessential Art Nouveau, Art Deco, or Arts and Crafts motifs.

Of secondary interest are pieces with bronze overlays these typically being Silver Crest. Such examples

A Heintz two-piece desk set, including a 2½" high inkwell/pen tray and a 3¼" high, 5" long letter rack/perpetual calendar. This set features a conventionalized fleur-de-lis sterling silver overlay on dark brown bronze. Production #1177.

are usually valued at about 25 percent less than comparable sterling on bronze items, and collectors prefer these bronze on bronze wares to be of superior design.

The quality of these overlays runs the entire gamut from the insipid to the inspired, and should be seriously considered when evaluating a potential purchase.

Size: This is somewhat of a relative factor in that medium to small examples of Heintz and Silver Crest with exceptional patinas, forms, and/or overlays are more valuable than large items with weak decorative aspects.

Large bronze wares with great designs and patinas are, of course, worth a premium.

As an afterword, it is essential to explain that Heintz wares seem to be more popular with collectors than Silver Crest items, and are usually priced 20 to 30 percent higher. Consequently, good examples of Silver Crest are often available at bargain prices. Investing in Silver Crest at this time is recommended, since prices are certain to increase.

Once the personal property of a Heintz craftsman, this extremely rare trophy cup is decorated with relief-carved figures and scenes in the bronze. 12¾" high, 10" wide.

Chapter Five
Heintz Art Metal Rarity Chart

During their heyday of the pre-Depression 1900s, both the Heintz Art Metal Shop and the Smith Metal Arts Company (Silver Crest) were prodigious firms, manufacturing a wide array of decorative and utilitarian bronze items.

Highly collectible today, some Heintz and Silver Crest items are scarce and elusive. Much of this has to do with the fact that objects such as lamps, jewelry, and large decorative wares were expensive when they were initially produced and simply would not have been made in the same quantity as incidental and inexpensive things like desk pieces and ashtrays.

A pair of Heintz cuff links and a watch fob. Both are unmarked.

Consequently, a structure of rarity exists for these items, which is detailed in the chart below.

Group One/ Common: smoking accessories, individual desk items, small bowls, vases, and trophies, card trays, and low candlesticks.

Group Two/ Relatively Rare: clocks, bookends picture frames, large bowls, vases, and trophies— especially those with green patinas, complete desk sets, small examples of jewelry such as bar pins, items made by The Art Crafts Shop, and small desk lamps.

Group Three/Rare: large table lamps, tall Tiffany-type candlesticks, fine examples of jewelry, and specially made non-production items.

Silver Crest bookends with sterling overlay of stylized sailing ships. 4¼" high, 3" wide. These bookends were commissioned by and marked "EDGEWATER BEACH HOTEL CHICAGO 1925— 1926".

Chapter Six

Heintz and Silver
Crest Photos and Prices

Vases and Bowls

Heintz vase with flared rim, gently sloping shoulders, and sterling floral overlay. 4½" high. Production #8810.

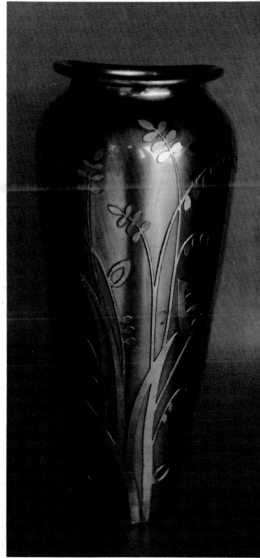

A Silver Crest vase with gently sloping shoulders and an upturned lip. Abstract organic overlay of bronze applied to a lightly patinated bronze surface. 12½" high. Production #41083.

Heintz baluster-form vase with everted rim and sterling silver open rose overlay. 12" high. Production #3617B.

Silver Crest corset-form vase with a streamlined bronze overlay of leafage, vines, and doves. 11¾" high. Production #41010.

Heintz vase with tapering cylindrical body and flared base and mouth. Sterling wild rose overlay. 12″ high.

Heintz cylinder vase with expanded foot and conventionalized organic overlay of sterling silver. 12″ high. Production #3543.

Unusual Silver Crest classical-form vases. Both exhibit textured surfaces with gold-plating. Bases are marked "GOLD INCRUSTED BRONZE." 7½" and 8" high. Production #2003 and #2005.

Opposite page:
Heintz vase with mottled green patina and sterling daisy design. 8" high. Production #3788.

Heintz vase with expanded cylinder body and sterling rose ornamentation. 5″ high. Production #3543B.

Heintz hourglass-form vase with sterling Thistle overlay. Silver-plating over bronze. The sterling overlay is tarnished black, thus providing the contrast which this type of finish usually lacks. 14½" high—a particularly large example of Heintz. Production #8709.

Heintz conical vase with heavy green patina and grape and leaf silver overlay. 8½" high.

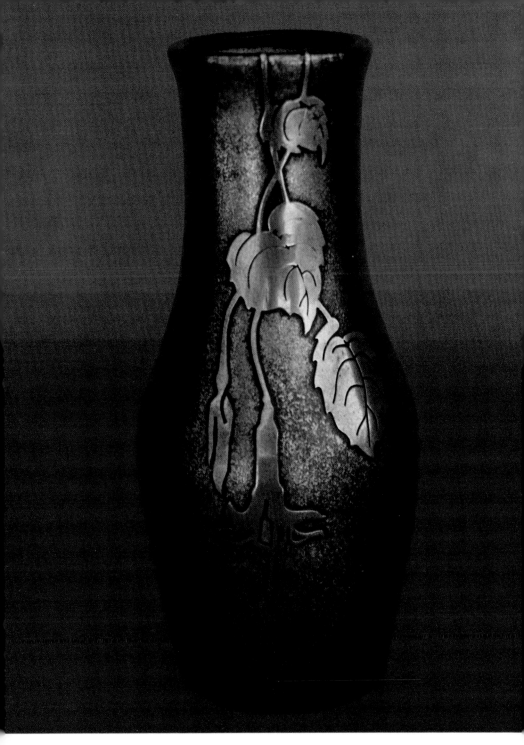

Silver Crest bronze vase with textured surface and bronze
Fuschia overlay. Production #C2008. 7¼″ high.

Heintz vase with wide mouth, tapering body, and bulbous base. Sterling daffodil overlay on stippled green bronze. 6½" high. Production #3670.

Heintz vase with oblate body and flared lip. Sterling floral decoration. 5" high. Production #3810B.

Top and side views of a Silver Crest compote which exhibits a textured, silver-plated surface and a sterling overlay of abstract fish and seaweed. 3" high, 7" diameter. Production #2053

Opposite page:
Silver Crest vase with lozenge-shaped body and pronounced lip and base. Vivid green patina with stylized floral ornamentation. 9½" high. Production #1016.

Top view of a large Silver Crest compote. The etched surface is silver-plated and highlighted with sterling pine cone and branch designs. 5 high, 8¾" wide. Production #2063.

Heintz low bowl with green patina and sterling pine branch overlay. 2" high, 9" diameter. Production #3706.

Opposite page:
Heintz baluster-form vase with glossy brown patina and flowing organic overlay of sterling silver. 12" high. Production #3708.

Opposite page:
Heintz vase with wide, pronounced rim, cylinder body, and angled base. This piece displays an exceptional silver overlay consisting of a pine tree and running water. 7½" high. Production #3596G.

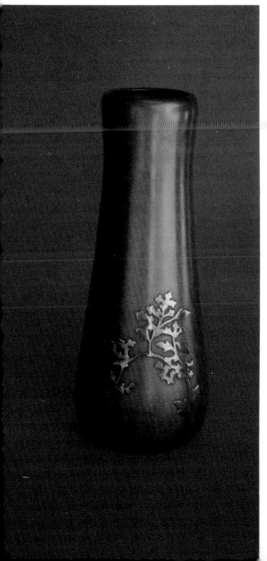

Heintz Art Metal vase cylindrical body with expanded mouth and streamlined sterling overlay, 11" high. Production #3831S.

Heintz tapered cylinder vase with gently angled mouth and base, and naturalistic sterling overlay. 8" high.

Opposite page:
Heintz vase with pronounced rim, and swollen, curvilinear body ornamented with a sterling palm tree. 6¼" high. Production #3661X.

Heintz cylinder vase with sterling hollyhock design. 6" high. Production #3668B.

Silver Crest cylinder vase with slightly swollen base and highly stylized carnation overlay. 6¾" high. Production #1094-1.

Silver Crest trumpet-form vase. Etched, silver-washed surface
with vertical sterling overlay of stylized flowers. 9¼″ high.
Production #2045.

A Silver Crest fruit bowl with rolled rim and deep, circular basin, supported by a saucer-form base. Wrap-around sterling organic design over coarse, silvered bronze. 4¾" high, 9¼" wide. Production #2068.

A wide-mouthed Heintz bowl with a compressed body and a sterling Art Nouveau overlay. 2" high, 8" diameter. Production #3589.

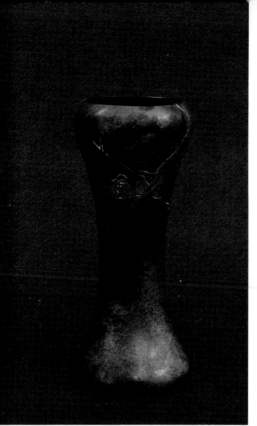

Opposite page:
Heintz cylinder vase embellished with sterling daffodils. 9" high.

Heintz hourglass-form vase of solid bronze, which has been plated with silver and overlaid with a sterling love-bird motif. 6¼" high. Production #3744.

Heintz urn-shaped vase with flared mouth and Greek key overlay. 7" high.

An attractive Heintz cylinder
vase with a wide rim and a
green "frogskin" patina. 6"
high. Production #3581C.

A bronze bowl with shouldered rim and modernistic sterling floral overlay. The base of this bowl is marked "SMACo" (Smith Metal Arts Co.) 2" high, 11" diameter. Production #900

This Silver Crest vase is, in all likelihood, an experimental piece, as it lacks the typical decorative overlay and is deeply acid-etched. 7¼" high.

A small Heintz hourglass-shaped vase with a pronounced rim and a daffodil overlay. 4" high. Production #3651C.

Desk Items

Silver Crest card tray with textured surface and geometric sterling silver overlay. Overall golden brass finish. 5¾″ diameter. Production #2105.

Silver Crest desk unit consisting of a pen tray, a stamp well, and a pair of inkwells which are concealed beneath hinged lids. Solid bronze with geometric bronze overlays and brass plating. Textured surface was achieved by sandblasting. 1¾″ high, 9¾″ long, 6½″ wide. Production #2213.

Two piece Silver Crest bronze desk set, consisting of a combination letter rack/perpetual calendar (3¾" high, 4" long) and a lidded inkwell (2½" high). Note the linear design work highlighted in a varying shade of bronze. Production #134.

A Silver Crest letter rack/perpetual calendar made from dark brown patinated bronze, highlighted with a contrasting bronze overlay of conventionalized organics. 3¾" high, 5¾" long, 1¾" wide. Production #173.

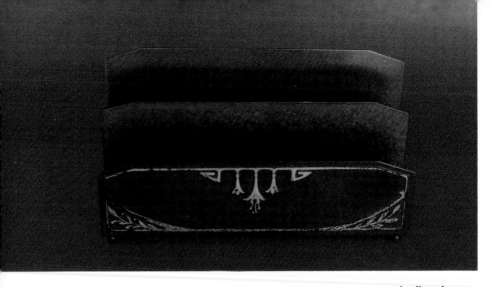

Silver Crest two-tier letter rack with Art Nouveau style floral overlay of sterling silver. 3¾" high, 7½" long, 2½" wide. Production #104.

Heintz six-piece desk set with sterling silver band applied to each item. As is often the case with Heintz, each of the overlays is actually marked "STERLING" in small block letters. This set consists of an inkwell (2½" high, 4" long), a stamp box (1¾" high, 3" long), a letter opener (10" long), a pen tray (9½" long), a rocker blotter (5½" long), and a perpetual calendar (3¾" high). All items marked with the Heintz diamond insignia except for the rocker blotter and the letter opener. Production #1096.

Heintz letter holder/calendar with conventionalized sterling floral design applied to variegated green bronze. 4" high, 4" long, 1¾" wide. Production #1175E. The impressed maker's mark is on the back of this piece, while the bottom bears an original paper label.

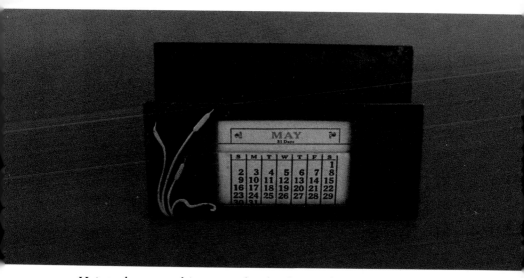

Heintz letter rack/perpetual calendar with green patina and sterling cattail overlay. 3½" high, 6" long, 2" wide. Production #1168.

Silver Crest card tray with sterling overlay of holly. 5¾"
diameter. No mark.

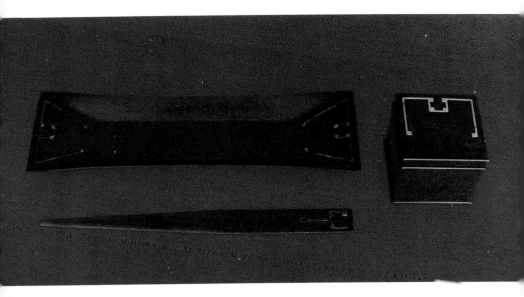

Heintz three piece desk set with silver Arts and Crafts motif on
dark brown bronze. This set consists of a pen tray (9¾" long, 3⅛"
wide), a letter opener (9" long), and an inkwell (2" high, 2¼"
square). Of the three pieces, only the letter opener is unmarked.
Production #1154.

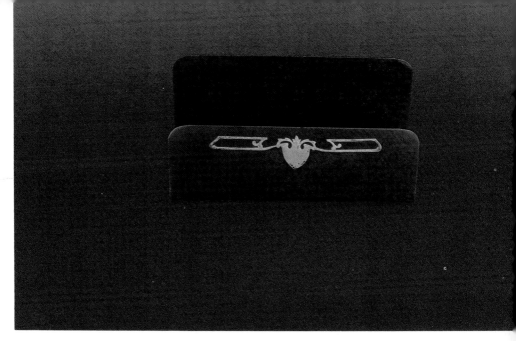

Heintz letter rack with applied sterling medallion. 3" high, 5½" long. No mark.

Heintz letter rack/perpetual calendar with a bold linear/geometric overlay of sterling silver. 5" high, 9" long, 3" wide. Production #1805.

Heintz bookends, sterling cattail design applied to variegated green bronze. 5¾" high, 3" wide. Production #7090D.

A Silver Crest perpetual calendar with textured silverplated bronze surface and stylized pine cone and branches sterling overlay. 3″ high, 3½″ wide.

Heintz five piece desk set, sterling silver lovebird overlay on dark brown bronze. Included in the set are a pen tray (6″ long), an inkwell (2¼″ high), letter opener (8¼″ long), a rocker blotter (5″ long), and a letter rack/perpetual calendar (4″ high, 4″ long). The only item bearing the Heintz mark in this set is the letter rack/calendar. Production #1175A.

Silver Crest desk items, including a perpetual calendar (3¼"
high) and a rocker blotter (4¾" long). The decorative overlay
consists of simple sterling linework.

Heintz three-piece desk set, comprised of an inkstand/pen tray
(2½" high, 8¾" long, 6" wide), a rocket blotter (5¼" long), and a
letter opener (11" long). Flowing Art Nouveau style overlay on
green bronze. Only the inkstand is marked. Production #1187B.

Silver Crest inkwell with large, bulbous body, domed lid, and a bronze overlay of naturalistic organic forms. 4½" high. No mark.

Heintz letter rack of strong overall Arts and Crafts design. This item lacks the usual overlay of sterling silver. 4¼" high, 8" long. Production #1074.

Heintz letter rack with silver plating and sterling floral overlay embellished with glass insets. Production #1155.

Heintz desk items, made from green patinated bronze with sterling Bluet applique. The blotter is 8½" long, and the perpetual calendar is 3¾" high, 4¾" wide. Production #1150B.

These unusual Heintz bookends display a sterling jungle scene on a silvered background, which is bordered by bronze. 4¼" high, 6" wide. Production #7202.

Heintz pentagonal-form bookends with a sterling parrot overlay. 5½" high, 4¼" wide. Production #7200.

A Heintz double inkwell/pen tray of simple, functional design. This piece exhibits a strong Frank Lloyd Wright/Prairie School influence. 3" high, 14" long. Production #1184.

A large Heintz desk set, which includes the following items: a letter rack (4" high, 6" long); an inkwell (2" high, 2½" square); a perpetual calendar (3½" high, 4½" wide); a pen tray (10" long); a rocker blotter (5½" long); a letter opener (9" long); and a set of four blotter corners (each 3¾" long). Undecorated wares such as this desk set usually represent transitional production from Arts Crafts Shop to Heintz Art Metal Shop manufacturing. Production #1000.

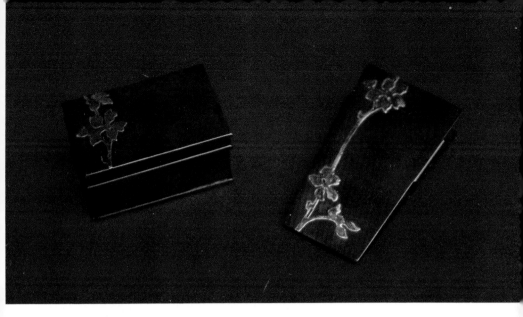

These scarce Heintz desk items include a stamp box (1½″ high, 2½″ long, production #1003) and a paper clip (3½″ long, no marks).

An unusually large Silver Crest inkwell/pen holder with marbled green patina and strong geometric sterling ornamentation. 4″ high, 7″ square. Production #110A.

Heintz four-piece desk set with a thick, mottled greenish brown patina and a sterling bamboo pattern overlay. Among the items in this set are a letter rack (4" high, 7½" long), a pen tray (9½" long), an inkwell (2¼" high, 4" long), and a stamp box (1½" high, 3" long). Production #109.

Heintz inkwell in a truncated pyramid form. 2" high, 5" square base. Unmarked.

A nicely designed Heintz Art Metal rocker blotter with ornate sterling linework on the top. 6½" long. Production #1099.

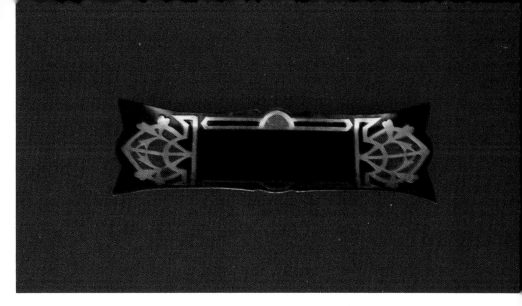

A stunning pen tray embellished with sterling and multicolored enamel. This piece was made by The Art Crafts Shop of Buffalo, New York, which was the forerunner of the Heintz Shop. 8¼" long.

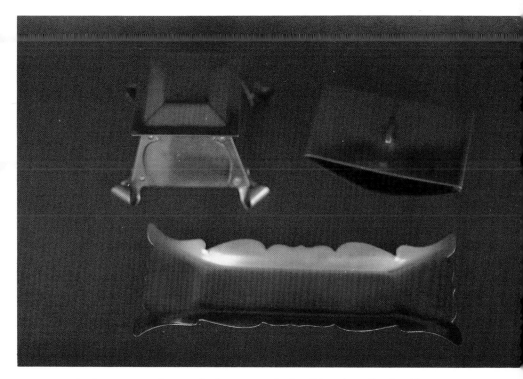

A three piece brass desk set made by The Art Crafts Shop. Unmarked.

Lighting

Silver Crest candlesticks with flared, sloping bases and widely rimmed sockets. Sterling silver overlay of leafage, golden wash over textured bronze. 9½" high. Production #C2152.

A beautiful Heintz table lamp with adjustable helmet shade. Vivid green patina with geometric sterling ornamentation. 13" high. No mark.

A Silver Crest dome-form desk lamp with polished bronze surface and sterling embellishment on the shade. 8½" high. No mark.

Heintz candlestick with tapered, circular base and flared socket. Silver-plated bronze with sterling rose and thorn ornamentation. 4¾" high. Production #871.

Heintz candlestick with dark brown patina contrasted with a sterling floral overlay. 5″ high. Production #3128B.

This pair of Heintz late production candlesticks features a textured, silver-plated surface which closely copied the Silver Crest line. Rarely encountered, it was probably a last-minute effort to compete with the Smith Metal Arts Company. 5½″ high. Production #31085

A large and impressive Heintz table lamp. The bronze base is decorated with a sterling bamboo design, while the removable shade is solid bronze with matching bamboo openwork. The interior of the shade was originally lined with silk. 18″ high, 16″ greatest shade diameter. No mark.

A Heintz candlestick very much in the style of Tiffany Studios. Saucer-form base with geometric sterling overlay, long and graceful turned bronze shaft, and tulip-shaped socket. 14″ high, 6″ basal diameter.

A Heintz Art Metal lamp with a footed base and a flared, dome-form bronze shade. Both the top and the bottom of the lamp are embellished with sterling floral overlays. 11" high. Unmarked.

A Heintz candlestick with floriform socket and intricate sterling overlay. This particular example is 6½" high, but was also made in a taller version which is pictured elsewhere. Unmarked.

A small Heintz desk lamp with adjustable helmet shade and sterling goldenrod overlay. 10" high. Unmarked, except for the original retailer's paper label, which reads "WUNDERLY BROS, FINE ART DEALERS, PITTSBURGH, PA."

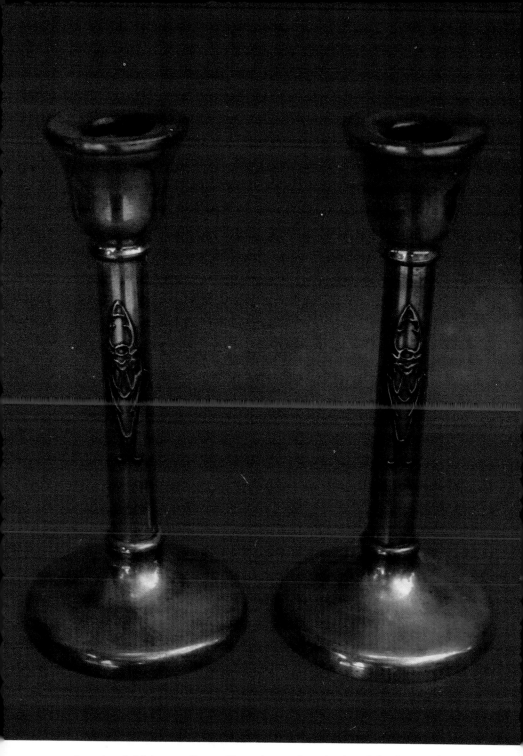

A pair of Heintz tall candlesticks with cylindrical bodies and flared sockets and bases. 8" high. Production #3126.

A Heintz Art Metal desk lamp with a circular base surmounted by a tapered cylinder body to which is attached harp-form arms supporting an adjustable helmet-type shade. A striking sterling overlay is contrasted against dark brown bronze. 13″ high. A Heintz Art Metal Shop paper label is found on the bottom of this lamp, while one of the shade arms bears the impressed retailer's mark of Macy's.

A highly desirable Heintz lamp which exhibits an exquisite green patina and an Oriental-style design. Note that the cut-out spider-web motif on the shade is repeated in sterling on the base. The shade is lined with gold silk. 10" high, 8½" greatest shade diameter.

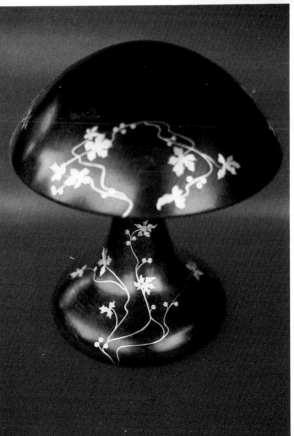

A large Heintz mushroom-form table lamp of graceful proportions. Both the base and the shade are heavily decorated with sterling leaf and vine motifs. 17" high, 14½" greatest shade diameter.

A Heintz table lamp with a tapered conical shade with cutout designs which are highlighted by interior silk lining. The designs on the shade are duplicated in sterling on the base of the lamp. 16" high. Unmarked.

Smoking Accessories

Heintz cigar bucket with a sterling overlay of the initials "O H S." Personalized pieces such as this are not considered to be very desirable by collectors. No production number, as this would have been a specially commissioned item.

Heintz smoking set comprised of a cigarette box with hinged lid and a nest of three ashtrays. This piece is embellished with a particularly strong geometric sterling overlay. 2" high, 8" long, 3½" wide. Production #8689.

A beautiful Silver Crest humidor of modernistic form with a glossy brown finish and golden bronze overlays of flying ducks. 6½" high, 4" diameter. No production number, but the retailer's mark of "Roos Bros CALIFORNIA" is present.

Heintz ashtray/matchbox holder with attached cigarette rests and removable glass liner. Sterling linear overlay. 4½" high, 9" diameter, Production #2644B.

Silver Crest bronze smoking set with ashtray and lidded cigarette box. Bronze mallard duck overlay. 2¼" high, 8¼" long, 4¼" wide. Production #495-W.

Heintz combination matchbox holder/ashtray with applied sterling design. 5¼" high. Production #2605.

Heintz cigarette box. Sterling floral overlay with blue glass insets and overall silver plating. 2" high, 4¾" long, 3½" wide. No mark.

Front and back views of a Silver Crest bronze humidor with highly stylized American Indian motif overlays. The back of this humidor is engraved as follows: "4th Specialty Show, Shepherd Dog Club of the West, S.F. Calif. April 2-3-26, Mr. J. Dupon, Trophy For Best Open." 7" high, 5" diameter. Production #2487.

Heintz Art Metal sterling and bronze cigarette box with attached matchbox holder. Strong, futuristic design. 3" high, 10" long, 4" wide.

A Heintz cigarette box with sterling linework and geometrics on the lid. 3" high, 8½" long, 3½" wide. Production #4095K.

Heintz lidded humidor with glass liner and strong silver Arts and
Crafts design on dark green bronze. 7″ high, 5½″ basal diameter.
Production #2647.

A Silver Crest smoking box shown opened and closed. This well designed piece opens to reveal an ashtray as well as a cigarette and matchbox holder. 2" high, 4¼" square.

Heintz cigarette box with sterling Arts and Crafts overlay on mottled green bronze. 1¼" high, 4½" long, 3½" wide.

Silver Crest "rocketship" form humidor with textured surface.
Note the absence of decorative overlays on this sleek modernistic
piece. 8½" high. Production #2636.

A Silver Crest sterling on bronze ashtray/matchbox holder. 3" high. Production #447.

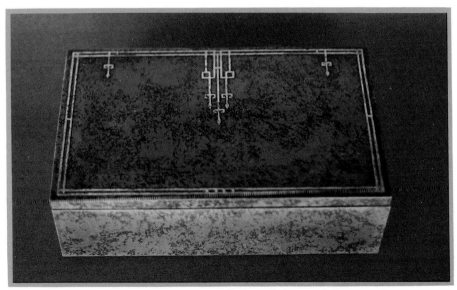

Heintz Art Metal bronze cigar box with beautiful green patina and an attractive geometric sterling silver overlay. 3" high, 10" long, 6" wide. Production #4090R.

Heintz ashtray with cigarette rest and sterling overlay portraying a hunting dog and a pheasant. 1¾" high, 6¼" diameter. Production #2652.

Heintz smoking set consisting of a 2¼" high match holder and a 3¼" high cigarette cup. Solid bronze with a conventionalized arrow overlay. Production #2500B.

Heintz ashtray with central nest of lift-out trays. 4″ diameter.

Heintz nested ashtray with sterling duck and organic overlay. 4″ diameter.

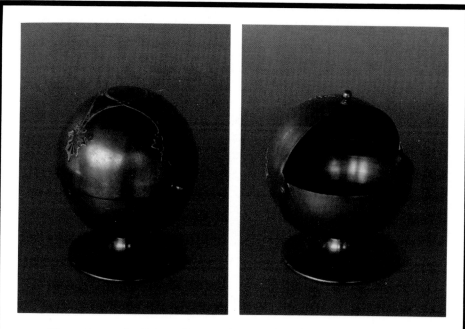

Two views of a Silver Crest ashtray/silent butler with a footed base and a spherical, hinged body. Sterling overlay on the top. 4½" high.

Heintz sterling and bronze matchbox holders. 2¼" long, 2" wide. No marks.

A Silver Crest bronze-on-bronze cigarette box with medieval knight motif. 1½" high, 4¼" long, 3½" wide. Production #2252-06.

A Silver Crest two-tone bronze cigarette cup with a Scotty dog overlay. 2" high. Production #411-H.

A Heintz cigarette box with a curving sterling design on the lid. 2½" high, 4¾" long, 3½" wide. Production #4073.

This Heintz cigarette box is unusual not only for the gold Tiffany-type patina, but also for the overlay which depicts a butterfly extracting nectar from a flower. 2½" high, 5" square. Production #4104.

Heintz two-sided cigarette box with attached handle and hinged lids. 4" high, 8" long, 3½" wide. Production #4100

A Heintz lidded tobacco jar with a sterling overlay of flowing organics and the initials "HWC." 5" high, 6½" diameter. Production #2613.

Rarities and Miscellaneous

An unengraved Silver Crest trophy/loving cup with a polished bronze surface and a sterling silver Art Deco style overlay. 14½" high, 14½" wide—this is an unusually large example of Silver Crest. Production #1301-14.

An unusual Silver Crest polished bronze kitchen timer. 4¼" high, 4½" wide. Production #125-36.

A Silver Crest electric clock with a geometric case made from polished bronze and German silver. Seth Thomas works and abstract numbering on the clock face. 4¼" high, 10¼" long, 3¼" wide. Production #925-924.

A Silver Crest picture frame made from textured bronze and embellished with a bronze overlay consisting of linework and stylized organics. 11″ high, 8″ wide. Unmarked except for the impressed production #2357-9.

Heintz trophy/loving cup with polished brass liner and overlay of flowing silver linework. This particular item was manufactured in three different sizes, of which this was the middle size. 7¼" high. Production #6545.

Opposite page:
A Heintz trophy vase with linear sterling overlay and an applied seal/medallion of "THE COUNTRY CLUB OF NEW BEDFORD INC. 1902." 10" high. Production #3598D. Also marked on the base is the retailer's name: "N.G. WOOD & SON."

Heintz handled bowling trophy with applied sterling linework. It is engraved as follows: "Union League Bowling Tournament, 1918-1919, Winning Team Quails, E.S. BULKLEY." 5½" high. Production #6586.

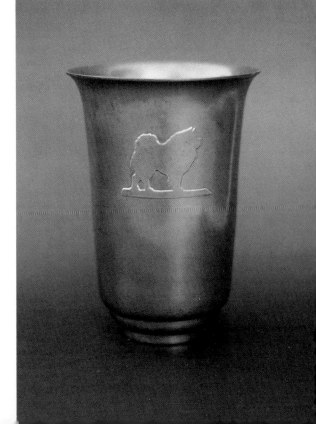

Silver Crest unengraved dog trophy with polished bronze surface and bronze chow overlay. 6¾" high. Production #1032.

Heintz picture frame with scrolled openwork and oval center. 3¼" high, 3" wide. No mark.

Heintz trophy cup, engraved for the "Governor's Cup Tournament,1925, Runner-Up, FIRST FLIGHT." Also present is the applied seal of "THE KERNWOOD COUNTRY CLUB. SALEM MASS." Attached angular handles and geometric sterling band. 5¾" high, 11½" greatest diameter. Production #1868.

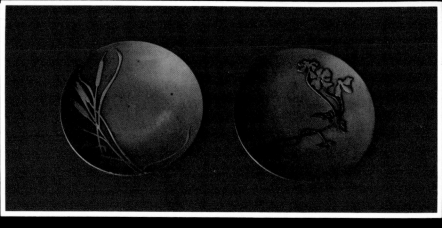

Small Heintz dishes with reddish patinas and sterling overlays of organic forms. Each is 4" in diameter. The dish on the right bears the production #544.

Heintz trophy cup with a sterling overlay of a hunter shooting a gun. 5½" high. The bottom of this piece is impressed with the words "PAT APD FOR" which is the pre-Heintz Shop transitional mark.

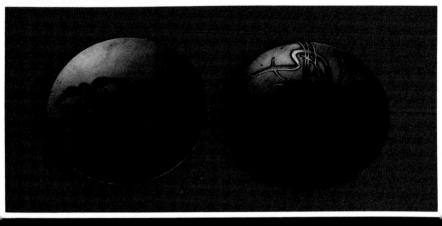

Heintz dishes with golden brown patinas and sterling seagull and wheat overlays. Each is 4" in diameter. No production numbers.

A beautifully designed Heintz trophy cup with sterling organic overlay. It is engraved "REVOLVER MATCH, BOARD OF OFFICERS, 65TH INS. NG-NY 1913, WON BY 1ST LIEUT. PAUL MALONE." 7" high. Production #6522.

A graceful Heintz trophy cup engraved "NEW YORK CREDIT
MENS ASSOCIATION, SEPTEMBER 29 1921, THIRD
ANNUAL GOLF TOURNAMENT AT HACKENSACK, WON
BY RICHARD S. DAVIS." Attached enamelled medallion. 11"
high. Production #6612.

A Heintz picture frame with a geometric sterling overlay on silvered bronze. This type of finish is referred to in Heintz catalogues as "French Gray." 7¾" high, 5¾" wide. Production #2127.

This clock is one of the most elusive items produced by the Heintz Art Metal Shop. 4" high, 4" wide. Production #1162.

A small Heintz trophy cup with a streamlined silver overlay. It is engraved: "ALL NUTLEY TENNIS CHAMPIONSHIP 1923, MENS SINGLES, WON BY PHILIP E. REDMOND." Trophies such as this constituted a large portion of the Heintz Shop's business. 6" high. Production #6535B.

A circular Heintz tray with recessed interior and sterling ornamentation on the edge. 10" diameter. Production #2562A.

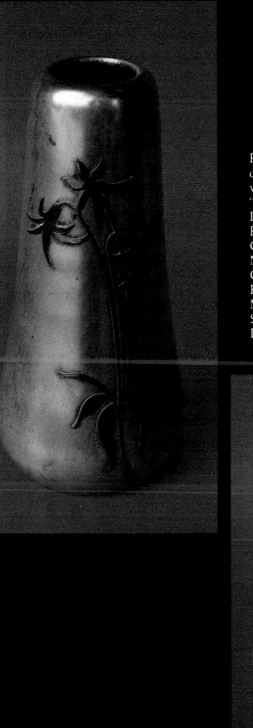

Front and back views of a Heintz trophy vase with silver or "French Gray" finish. It is engraved: "CALIFORNIA HOTELS CO., GUESTS TOURNAMENT, LADIES CHAMPIONSHIP FLIGHT, WINNER, MISS GLADYS SELICK." 6¾" high. Production #3641.

An Art Crafts Shop plate with embossed designs circling the edge. 7" diameter. Unmarked.

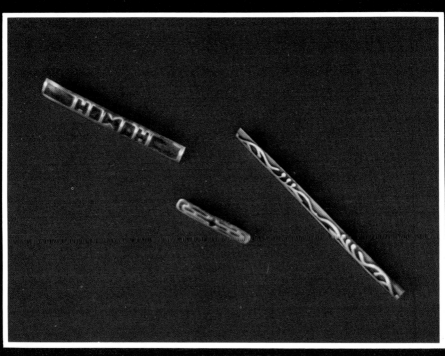

A grouping of Heintz sterling and bronze bar pins. All are unmarked, which is typically the case.

Chapter Seven
Original Advertisements

The following selection of original black and white advertisements are reprinted from a circa 1916 Heintz Art Metal Shop catalogue. These pictures and their descriptions offer additional insight as regards the identification of specific patterns, rarely encountered production items such as #2513—a complete four-piece smoker set, as well as various facts and details as furnished by the Heintz Shop itself.

During their heyday, the Heintz Art Metal Shop marketed and distributed their wares throughout the country, accomplished in part by ads such as these which ran in appropriate publications of the era, including Gustav Stickley's magazine *The Craftsman*.

No. 526—Tray

On this tray the silver is confined to one-half of the space, the balance being plain, and showing the beauty of the finishes we employ most attractively.

The Heintz process (patented) causes the silver and bronze to fuse at point of contact, the silver ornamentation thus being permanently applied.

Diameter, 6 inches.

No. 446—Tray

This tray is decorated with silver-leaf design, the leaves being hand engraved to show the detail.

The silver-on-bronze method of making art wares is original with us, and the effect obtained is different from any other art wares made.

Diameter, 7 inches.

No. 2113—Frame

THIS frame has oval opening, and comes in size 9 x 7.

Frame is artistically ornamented with silver.

Silver-on-bronze frames invariably display a photograph to excellent advantage.

No. 3584A—Vase

THIS is a small vase of symmetrical design, is 3½ inches high, and has silver ornamentation as illustrated.

Makes an appropriate, moderate-priced, gift for any purpose.

The vase comes in a variety of silver decorations.

No. 3585B—Vase

THIS vase has California Pepper ornamentation in silver, and stands 3½ inches high. It is a very good vase for small bouquets.

Makes a desirable card, or other, prize.

Several other effective silver decorations can be had on shape illustrated.

Horse Chestnut Leaf.

Narcissus.

Woodbine.

No. 3601 B — Vase

THE proportions of this vase are more on the order of a jardiniere. It is 7¾ inches high, and is quite a large vase. The bamboo design contrasts effectively with the bronze background.

Other designs applied on this form vase are Woodbine, Poppy, Pepper Tree, and Wisteria.

No. 3603 B — Vase

STANDING 9 inches high, and being of symmetrical proportions, this vase is very desirable. It has attractive silver ornamentation as shown.

Heintz designs are of exceptional merit, and all articles are of graceful form, as in the case of the vase illustrated herewith.

No. 3617 A — Vase

BEING 12 inches high, this is one of our taller vases, and has silver ornamentation running the entire length.

The designs based on floral motif, which form the silver ornamentation of many Heintz Vases, are particularly appropriate for an article intended as a container of flowers.

No. 3618A—Vase

ANOTHER of the taller vases, also 12 inches high. The Pussy Willow design in silver is very appropriate for the simple lines of this vase.

Silver ornamentation is equally effective when applied in the form of a simple design, as illustrated on No. 3618A Vase. The designs which are simple are, of course, less expensive than the designs with considerable detail to them.

No. 4075—Cigar Box

THIS is decorated with Oak Leaf design applied in sterling silver. It holds one box of fifty cigars.

The ornamentation is of a style that appeals to masculine taste, and the box is of substantial construction.

Heintz Smokers' articles invariably make appreciated gifts.

Dimensions, 10 inches x 6 inches x 3 inches.

No. 2558—1066—Tobacco Jar

IS of substantial-weight bronze, and is very well made. The silver is applied in the Forget-Me-Not design, matching No. 1066 desk set.

This tobacco jar is of such superior appearance it is sure to please the most exacting man.

5 inches high, 4 inches diameter.

No. 2513—Smoker Set

Consists of ash bowl, cigar bowl, cigarette bowl, match bowl, and tray. The articles are made of a good weight of bronze, and the set is very compact and complete.

This is our standard set, and is decorated with numerous other designs.

Diameter of tray, 8⅜ inches.

No. 1861A—Nut Bowl

This nut bowl is of simple design, with ornamentation of silver which is both artistic and in conformity with the simplicity of the bowl itself.

Another nut bowl is shown on cover—one of a number of attractive shapes, suitably decorated

No. 7091—Book Ends

These book ends are of somewhat smaller proportions, but are equally serviceable, and are preferred by some to the larger book ends.

Smaller book ends frequently look well where the larger size would be out of proportion, and in such cases the book ends illustrated would answer nicely.

6 inches high, 2¾ inches wide.

No. 7090—Book Ends

THE shape of these book ends differ from No. 7091, but the articles are of approximately the same size.

The decoration is a floral design in silver.

6 inches high, 2⅞ inches wide.

No. 5504B—Electric Lamp

THIS lamp is 14½ inches high, and has silver ornamentation in the form of a Grape Leaf design.

The shade is adjustable, and may be tilted, so as to reflect the light where wanted.

It is a thoroughly practical as well as ornamental lamp.

This has proved to be a very popular lamp.

No. 5503B—Electric Lamp

THIS is an exceptionally handsome lamp. The shade is lined with silk of good quality. The base of lamp is decorated with sterling silver. The shade is pierced bronze.

The dimensions of lamp are as follows:

Height,	18 inches.
Diameter of base,	6¼ inches.
Lower diameter of shade,	16 inches.

Woodbine design.

Bibliography

Johnson, Bruce. *The Official Identification and Price Guide to Arts and Crafts,* New York: House of Collectibles, 1988

Ludwig, Coy L. *The Arts and Crafts Movement in New York State 1890s—1920s,* Layton, Utah: Peregrine Smith, 1983,

McConnell, Kevin. "The Heintz Art Metal Shop's Great Bronze Age." *The Antique Trader Price Guide to Antiques,* August, 1990

White, Dave. "A Nearly Forgotten Maker of Memories." *Buffalo News Magazine,* April 11, 1982

"Another Metal Shop Makes Its Mark." *Buffalo News Magazine,* August 1, 1982